Animals
and Their
Senses

ANIMAL SIGHT

by Kirsten Hall

Reading consultant: Susan Nations, M.Ed.,
author/literacy coach/consultant

WR WEEKLY READER
EARLY LEARNING LIBRARY

Please visit our web site at: www.earlyliteracy.cc
For a free color catalog describing Weekly Reader® Early Learning Library's list
of high-quality books, call 1-877-445-5824 (USA) or 1-800-387-3178 (Canada).
Weekly Reader® Early Learning Library's fax: (414) 336-0164.

Library of Congress Cataloging-in-Publication Data

Hall, Kirsten.
    Animal sight / Kirsten Hall.
      p. cm. — (Animals and their senses)
    Includes bibliographical references and index.
    ISBN 0-8368-4803-9 (lib. bdg.)
    ISBN 0-8368-4809-8 (softcover)
    1. Vision—Juvenile literature. I. Title.
  QP475.7.H34   2005
  573.8'8—dc22   2005046182

This North American edition first published in 2006 by
Weekly Reader® Early Learning Library
A Member of the WRC Media Family of Companies
330 West Olive Street, Suite 100
Milwaukee, WI 53212 USA

Copyright © 2006 by Nancy Hall, Inc.

Weekly Reader® Early Learning Library Editor: Barbara Kiely Miller
Weekly Reader® Early Learning Library Art Direction: Tammy West
Weekly Reader® Early Learning Library Graphic Designer and Page Layout: Jenni Gaylord

Photo Credits
The publisher would like to thank the following for permission to reproduce their royalty-free photographs:
AbleStock: 4, 5, 11, 12, 13, 15, 19, 21; Corel: 18; Digital Vision: Cover, title page, 6, 7, 8, 9, 10, 14, 16, 20;
Fotosearch/It Stock Free: 17

Printed in the United States of America

1 2 3 4 5 6 7 8 9 09 08 07 06 05

Note to Educators and Parents

Reading is such an exciting adventure for young children! They are beginning to integrate their oral language skills with written language. To encourage children along the path to early literacy, books must be colorful, engaging, and interesting; they should invite the young reader to explore both the print and the pictures.

Animals and Their Senses is a new series designed to help children read about the five senses in animals. In each book young readers will learn interesting facts about the bodies of some animals and how the featured sense works for them.

Each book is specially designed to support the young reader in the reading process. The familiar topics are appealing to young children and invite them to read — and reread — again and again. The full-color photographs and enhanced text further support the student during the reading process.

In addition to serving as wonderful picture books in schools, libraries, homes, and other places where children learn to love reading, these books are specifically intended to be read within an instructional guided reading group. This small group setting allows beginning readers to work with a fluent adult model as they make meaning from the text. After children develop fluency with the text and content, the book can be read independently. Children and adults alike will find these books supportive, engaging, and fun!

— Susan Nations, M.Ed., author, literacy coach, and consultant in literacy development

People see with their eyes. Our eyes see colors, sizes, and shapes.

Our eyes send **messages** to our brains. Then our brains tell us what we are seeing.

A snake has an eye on each side of its head. It can see things well only if they are close.

Eagles have large eyes for their small heads. They can see small objects and colors very well.

A frog's eyes stick out from its head.
Frogs can see in all directions.

Eagles have large eyes for their small heads. They can see small objects and colors very well.

A frog's eyes stick out from its head.
Frogs can see in all directions.

A **chameleon** can see things in
different places at the same time.
Each eye moves on its own.

Chimpanzees are like people. They see the world around them in many colors.

Owls cannot see many colors.
The things they see look black,
white, or gray.

Birds can see things better than people can. Many birds can see colors very well, too.

Cats can see about six times better than people can in very little, or **dim**, light.

tentacle

A snail's eyes are on the ends of its top **tentacles**. A snail can see in all directions, but it cannot see things well.

eye spot

A sea star has an eye spot on the end
of each of its arms. These spots tell the
sea star if it is in a dark or light place.

Spiders can have up to eight eyes.
Most spiders can tell if it is light or
dark around them. But they cannot
see very well.

Bees have two large eyes and three small eyes. Each large eye is made up of hundreds of little eyes.

A camel has long eyelashes. They keep blowing sand out of the camel's eyes. Eyelashes help camels see during sandstorms.

An alligator's eyes are on the top of its head. It can see above the water when it swims. Its body stays hidden while it hunts for **prey**.

Sight is important for most animals. A shark uses its sense of sight to find food

Sight helps a prairie dog look for
danger. Sight helps animals live
in the wild.

Glossary

chameleon — a small lizard that changes colors to match its surroundings

messages — information that is passed on in writing, by speaking, or by signals

prey — animals that are hunted and killed by other animals for food

tentacles — long, bendable parts that stick out from the heads of some animals

For More Information

Books

Animal Eyes. Look Once, Look Again (series).
David M. Schwartz (Gareth Stevens)

How Animals See Things. Rookie Read-About Science
(series). Allan Fowler (Children's Press)

Let's Look at Eyes. Let's Look at (series). Simona Sideri
(Smart Apple Media)

*Whose Eyes Are These? A Look at Animal Eyes — Big,
Round, and Narrow.* Whose Is It (series). Peg Hall
(Picture Window Books)

Web Sites

Those Eyes
www.greenscreen.org/newsletter/articlesjr/ThoseEyes.html
A newsletter for kids that explains how certain animals see

Index

About the Author

Kirsten Hall is an author and editor. While she was still in high school, she published her first book for children, *Bunny, Bunny*. Since then she has written and published more than eighty titles. A former teacher, Kirsten currently spends her days writing and editing and her evenings tutoring. She lives in New York City with her husband.